The Ob Arvon I⌣⌣⌣⌣ Collection

Winning poems from the
Arvon Poetry Competition 1993

jointly sponsored by
The Observer
and
Duncan Lawrie Ltd

Selected by
**Eavan Boland, Gillian Clarke,
Liz Lochhead, Penelope Shuttle**

Produced by PD2 for the Observer

First published in Great Britain in 1994 by
Guardian Newspapers Limited
119 Farringdon Road London EC1R 3ER

ISBN 0852650329

Contents

Introduction

The poems in this collection are the prize-winners, and those selected for special commendation, from the seventh Arvon International Poetry Competition.

Entries were judged without the panel of judges knowing the identity of the competitors. We have arranged the poems in alphabetical order of their titles. Readers, if they wish, can make their own selection of winners before turning to where the names of the authors, and their prizes are listed. The winner received a prize of £5000, there are five prizes of £500, ten prizes of £250 each. There are a further fourteen poems that have been specially commended and are included in this collection.

There were over 13,000 entries for 1993's Arvon International Poetry Competition from which these winning poems, and special commendations, were selected by Eavan Boland, Gillian Clarke, Liz Lochhead and Penelope Shuttle.

The Arvon Foundation acknowledges with thanks the sponsorship provided by The Observer for the first prize, and by Duncan Lawrie Limited for the other fifteen prizes.

An African

Valerie Whitaker

You lost your name on the boat from Africa
In your mother's womb.
The slave-master was glad she was in calf
Hoped she'd die and that you'd live.
A fine black boy fetched more than a woman.
A little page boy, a curiosity.
Who would be your Oberon?

A slave to monarchs:
But when you came to man's estate,
You'd grown out of your velvet suit
And the swagger in your step caught the eyes of the girls
So mad George tired of you, sent you to the country.

But you kept your name.
How odd it sounded here:
Charles Bacchus, cup-bearer to the gods -
Or at least those in unimaginable London.
I suppose he thought you'd be safe here,
Grow into some ole' nigger settin' on the doorstep.
Didn't know you could die of loneliness,
And the way girls held their skirts so close
As they passed by you.

Animaculture

Hilary Llewellyn-Williams

The gardening angels tuck their robes
into their belts, pull their boots on
cover their heads with haloes and set out

to cultivate the world. Each one
has hoe and sickle, spade and watering-can
and wings, and a small patch

to care for. They come in all colours:
dawn, rain or dusk, rose, marigold,
moss, midnight; gliding between

reflections, rarely seen. At three
years old, occasionally I'd catch
the flick of a wing, a glitter on the air

a tickle of warmth behind me, someone there
playing roll-in-the-grass with me
pushing my swing. And at night

my gardening angel laid her head
beside me, smelling of daisies,
and breathed with me. At my maiden flight

along our street, my feet grazing the privet,
past lamp-posts and garden gates, her voice
in my ear steered me and said -

This is the way to heaven, along here.
Since then, so may false choices:
knotted with weeds, I'm overgrown

and parched as dust. Who will open
the door to the garden, who will water
me now? Wise child, I trust my own

right words, I knew the angel's name
and that death was part of the game.
I find it very hard to remember her.

The gardening angels prune and propogate
moving in secret through the soul's acres;
have I called on mine too late?

Whistling, she strolls in from long ago,
and she hands me the rake and hoe -
Your turn, she says; and I feel my wings stir.

Black Market

Graham Mort

It is dawn and the river steams;
he waits for you by the bridge - as they
said he would - his feet gently stamping
on the snow's crust, next to the chestnut-seller
and that news-vendor breathing smoke.

You sidle up to him, this zek-head
in the long coat: no salute,
you greet him with one word and hear
your own language harsh in his mouth.
No names, no pack-drill.

His eyes water in their red slits,
his lashes blinking at the cold or
at poverty; he licks a stained moustache,
his tongue furtive behind the cigarette.
Already his inattention cheats you.

You are wearing your good shoes, your
warm jacket, quilted against the cold
as your head is quilted against the hour
by last night's drinks: at the bar you boasted
of leaving, the whole city turning under your heel.

He thumbs the white crescents of his eyes;
a rat slicks across dead nasturtiums, sleek
as the river where it goes under the parapet;
the man gestures 'follow', his hand an exclamation,
his nails filthy with secret work.

He smells of wet wool, stale books, of dead
philosophy, of something you want or meant
to get round to in the end but never did:
he squats in your head and his name
cannot be written down or evicted, ever.

He is your blind date, waiting as you are:
you'll follow him into the city, into
basement cafes where the soup is thin and sour,
into tanyards and shopfronts where the deals
are struck; each one, someone's bad bargain.

Nothing goes as planned: one job you said,
wanting to be on a flight, counting dollars,
seeing a softly torn sea below, curving palms,
a catamaran far out and a beach-house where
cool women are sipping rum spilled over ice.

Now you've got packets hidden in the floor,
daren't answer the phone, or that late-night knock;
the landlady's eyes are black with sudden hate
and her face shows you what you are; today
you rang a friend and the line died.

Tonight they'll hand you an address, a bridegroom's
photograph: enough to know him at close range.
Something wrapped in oiled cloth, its chambers
clicking in your hand. Then used notes: half now and
half later. Then moments ticking themselves empty.

Blue Angel

Peter Burton

I

The light in this blue poem is the light of desire
for an absent object - space in the season
of pure relationship -
                        perspectives of an interior
landscape that owe nothing to reality
and therefore might possess the soul. Winter in Umbria.

            There are hyacinths here.
They are serious, for they would seem to understand
the space they inhabit - or possess.

            They are beautiful
because they do not, and their colours
are those of a Renaissance angel and insuperably given.

II

The light in this blue room is no longer mysterious.
Each hour I write is a shadow that walks ahead, only

to return with hyacinths from the future, perspectives
yet unborn. Reality is born here, an enlightenment.

Everything is space in this snow-bright dispensation -
rock and conifer, the last bones of nature coming up for
                                                        air.
There is something devout in their refusal

to obey oblivion as if their nerves had been burnt
and impassioned by the heresy of solitude.

III

These words are possessed by an ecstasy of the inward
gaze. The artist implies eternity in a looking-glass

gazing deeper in the passion of interiority. Hyacinths
flower on the horizon of her soul. A season
without a shadow. Reality is the Giotto angel in the
                                        hyacinth.

The blue in her eyes seems created only to reflect

but this not-human light is only the concept of light.
It bends like an angel relative to space alone -

contemplates itself, a virgin in a mirror, outside time
and so shadowless it is pungent to the eye.

Caliban's Books

Michael Donaghy

Hair oil, boiled sweets, chalk dust, squid's ink...
Bear with me. I'm trying to conjure my father,
age fourteen, as Caliban - picked by Mr Quinn
for the role he was born to play because
'I was the handsomest boy at school'
he'll say, straight-faced, at fifty.
This isn't easy. I've only half the spell,
and I won't be born for twenty years.
I'm trying for rainlight on Belfast Lough
and listening for a small blunt accent barking
over the hiss of a stove getting louder like surf.
But how can I read when the schoolroom's gone
black as the hold of a ship? Start again.

Hair oil, boiled sweets...
But his paperbacks are crumbling in my hands,
sea-changed bouquets, each brown page
scribbled on, underlined, memorized,
forgotten like used pornography:
The Pocket Treasury of English Verse
How to Win Friends and Influence People
30 Days to a More Powerful Vocabulary

Fish stink, pitch stink, seaspray, cedarwood...
I seem to have brought us to the port of Naples,
midnight, to a shadow below deck
dreaming of a distant island.
So many years, so many ports ago!
The moment comes. It slips from the hold
and knucklewalks across the dark piazza
sobbing, *maestro! maestro!* But the duke's long dead
and all his magic books are drowned.

The Chevy And The Pond

Derrek Hines

For some reason in memory they exchanged functions:
the pond was the wreck, gleaming like a hub-cap,
settled down on its flat whitewalls that were
cracked in the folds where air met water.

The '57 Chevy was limpid, dragonfly haunted,
quivering in the rain under the trees in the back lot
where they'd left it when its big end failed.
Everything was sub-aquatic in the green light,
the speedometer a depth gauge; through the delicate
lacy perforations of rust, weeds poked, goldenrod at
noon;
and every day the sun in the ruby tail light
as it braked in the dusk for night.
A place to meet and smoke.

Later when we were older and left, they broke the pond
for spares, and crushed the rest for scrap.

The Chevy they back-filled, along with the A & Ws
and the summers of heart-stopping rock and roll
that laid down those highways for us into forever.

A Childless Woman

Kerry Hardie

With young women I am motherly,
with older women, daughterly,
with women of my own age, lonely.

I

First a landscape smudged with sound and trickles of
                                                    sound.
Unfocused. Air threaded with rain.

Where the swollen river has loosed out its brown waters
into the unreachable marsh-places, and the shine
of the cold sky shows flatly in pieces and shapes of flood -
there the frogs grunt,

heave, flop about in watery eruptions,
quietening when they hear us,
'til only an old bull, quivering, out of his head with sex,
regards us balefully from his station
on a female, mostly submerged
in the spawny glub and not protesting.

It is all woven-woods, sounds, light;
before the frills and flutterings begin.
Everything here, but hidden. Mud-smell, frogs heaving,

and such profligacy of black-specked jel...
'How wasteful nature is', my husband says.

II

I have a part-time, not-mine son,
loaned from a woman that I never meet.

Sometimes I wonder if she thinks of me.

III

It is no big deal, happens over and over.
Just haunted, in Spring, by the grey women who have
                                                made me
walking endlessly in slow file from the past.
And I am them, and I am breaking the line.
This is what it means: the year the spring didn't come.
Spilled water, seeping underground.

This fragility: not mine, but the way I have
just now of perceiving the world.
A fragile time, February going into March.

IV

I am become a woman standing on the sidelines,
on station platforms meeting and seeing off trains,
casually surprised to be remembering
with gifts the anniversaries of friends' children.
A woman given
to speaking carefully, saying mostly the generous thing,
watching the brown flow of rivers, waiting
by windows open onto dusk.

Darlene's

Pansy Maurer-Alvarez

When I was a few years out of knee socks and saddle
　　　　　shoes, A-cups and Clearasil, I found myself
well into bell-bottoms and a date out on a Saturday, out
　　　　　in a pick-up, looking out for spare parts.

We stopped at DARLENE'S up near the interstate round
　　　　　about lunch. Now DARLENE'S
was a one-woman concern, except when her ageing mom
　　　　　came to help peel eggs.

Everyone around knew DARLENE'S; it's where you'd go
　　　　　after the movies with your girl-
friends or boyfriend and narrow your choice down to
　　　　　DARLENE'S Death-by-Chocolate, her

Peanut-butter Cheesecake, that made your tongue stick
　　　　　to the roof of your mouth for days on end, or
DARLENE'S Own Chocolate Mint Brownies, just about
　　　　　as black as her Death and so permeated

with mint, you could have used them for mouthwash;
　　　　　you'd have to start kissing real hard after
one of DARLENE'S mint brownies just to get the feeling
　　　　　back in you lips, tongue and taste buds.

DARLENE'S served such a hefty chowder you could
　　　　　stand your spoon up in it and you got plenty
of crackers along side. She herself was skin and bone,
　　　　　being a one-woman concern 6-days a week.

The oldies-but-goldies would go out for a sundae or a
　　　　　split in summer. Everybody ended up at
DARLENE'S at one point or other in life. But it wasn't
　　　　　really a family place because DARLENE'S

was small and always packed so you had to not be in a
            hurry for your food. My pick-up truck
guy ordered a sub. Now DARLENE'S were the biggest,
            longest, highest-piled

for miles around. You had to really work hard to get your
            mouth around one of DARLENE'S
subs. It was the kind of belch-accompanying
accomplishment men in my parts were real proud of.

I ordered a salad bowl. Not the *Gardener's Bowl*, that
            had the beets, corn, carrots, the tomatoes,
potatoes, peppers, onions and slaw on a deep bed of fresh
            lettuce, but DARLENE'S Own Special Bowl,

with the beets, carrots, corn, hard-boiled egg, the onions,
            peppers, potatoes, tomatoes and,
instead of slaw, a mound of Dairy Maid cottage cheese.
            The Dairy Maid van used to be out

in front of DARLENE'S lots, especially in summer when
            she could hardly keep up. That Saturday,
I looked down at my deep, luscious bowl, crowned with
            my favourite dairy product and there,

right in the middle of my pristine mound, like a cherry on
            the fluffy pinnacle of a DARLENE'S
Sundae, was the thickest, blackest, longest shiniest, pubic
            hair I had ever come into such close

contact with, out of context, that is. My spare-part date
            looked, then looked away; he had black hair.
I didn't, don't and never will, anywhere. The woman who
            ran DARLENE'S was a red-head dyed

somewhere between *Venetian Renaissance Copper* and
            Rich Oriental Plum, worked up into a high-rise
that shone like patent leather in a spotlight. Could this
            specimen have conceivably come from anywhere

20

on her pale, overworked body? Anyway, I was sure it was
                    male. So, where did it float in
from? Who
was hiding out in DARLENE'S kitchen? The puny Dairy
                    Maid man? Now we've all eaten a hair,

at one point or another, our own or the dog's, in the soup
            or the stew. Bet we've had fingernails, too,
no doubt in deep-fried crab cakes (although hardly at
                    DARLENE'S) and just thought they were

bits of shell. Could have even had their own dirt deep-
            fried along with them. Sitting at DARLENE'S
that Saturday round noon, I was imbued with my new-
            found, bra-less bravado; I manoeuvered my prize

hair onto my fork, raised it to my lips and closed my
            mouth, ever so licentiously, around it. It didn't
taste of anything. My date stared, mid-bite. My mother,
            who approved of DARLENE'S high standard

of hygiene, would have shrieked, 'Spit it out! Quick! You
            don't know where it's been!' Oh, but I did.
I knew exactly where it belonged, just not on whom.
There I was eating pubic hair in public and all I could

think of was what my mother would have said! *Spare
            Parts* started applying himself with extra vigour
to his DARLENE'S Super Sub, trying not to watch me
            munch and crunch around on my hair. Was I

proving too much of a woman for him? Right there in
one of DARLENE'S booths? Just as well his mouth
was stuffed with sub. But I was having a hard time; my
            hair wouldn't split either crosswise or lengthwise.

Male, I thought, so unbending (this, too was new-found).
            The woman we all called DARLENE came by
to ask if everything was okay. 'Great bowl,' I said. In the
                    end, of course, I swallowed the hair whole

because you can't turn around on a one-lane, one-way
        street, not at DARLENE'S, not anywhere. But
you can look back and I sometimes wonder if that hair in
all its shining tenacity wasn't female after all.

Down from Parnassus

in memory of A.R., plumber and trumpet-player

Alan Gibson Reid

1. Portrait

Time was he chain-smoked fifty fags a day,
sixty, sometimes, when the heat was on,
with a big job coming up and him not well.
He'd cough his guts out at the crack of dawn,
head-down in the kitchen-sink, while the kettle
was coming to the boil. For all of that,
he was proud of his physique, of his slim waist
that never gained an extra inch of fat
in over forty years. And still, at least,
he had his teeth, and a head of hair, though grey.

Post-war. No van. He'd lug-hump all his tools
by rusty bike; each morning, push-off
down the brae for a day's work; getting his hands wet
for next to nothing. Cess-pool, cattle-trough
attended to, he'd pech home with tired feet.
Recover fast. Tea, a wash and brush-up,
and it was time for the brass band practice,
with the cat following him to the bus-stop;
or, wearing his best suit, he'd be off to a dance,
back in the small hours on his stocking-soles,

often with cakes or fruit. He had the knack
of peppering the ear with triple-tongues.
But the garden was a wild place. He was lazy
about the house, after demob, his lungs
still in their first flush; and him uneasy,
living on his nerves, with a textbook neurosis
following active service. Changeable,
blue as a B-flat or ten degrees
over the moon and climbing: always able
to see the darker side when work was slack,

with no incentive to remove his slippers.
Irate. Lost-looking in his dungarees.
Barely nine stone of him. Corns on his feet,
and a debilitating touch of fibrositis
in his left shoulder. I'd rub in Deep Heat,
around the affected area, soothe the muscles
with light massage while he'd be loudly sharing
with all and sundry, his infirmities;
from lookers-in to see how he was faring,
to the fishwife from Arbroath come with the kippers.

2. The Burst Pipe

The hillside stretched
in a series of undulations,
shades of heather-mauve,
that mingled, ultimately,
with the blue blur
of the back hills

On the lower slopes,
beehives hummed
among silver birches.

We rolled up our sleeves.

He said,
'It's up there, someplace',
meaning a burst pipe
that was getting worse each day,
with mud, grit, and God knew what,
in the kitchen-tap.

We'd have our work cut out
in that wild expanse
and burgeoning of nature,
boulders in the way;
black-faced sheep looking boozed.

First thing was
to locate the leak -
knickety-knackety!

The old man pistol-held his dowsing-rods,
and marked out the line of supply
from the well-source at the hilltop
to the back of the house;
then hunted down the leak
to where the water bubbled,
escaping from the ground.

We did the spade-work, then,
digging down
to expose the pipe
for the full treatment
by a master-plumber -
the cutting, cleaning, soldering,
and fitting for the future;
with a break in the operation
for a quick cuppie;
the tea-water boiled in a pan,
in an instant, blowlamp-heated.
Brooke Bond added, brewed up,
then drunk down with the view.

The postman waved
from the road below.
And all day long,
a pair of cuckoos,
long-tailed, kestrel-like,
were cuckoo-calling
in the garden trees;
keeping us company
in the high glen, where, in winter,
the big deer come down
to the back door,
looking for hand-outs
when the ground is hard,
food scarce, hunger over-riding
their basic fear
of human habitation.

It was years since the old man
had learned the dowsing trick.
He'd learned the technique from a farm-worker,
at a farm, once,
where he'd fixed an outside spiggot
that a cow,
liking the smooth-soothe of it,
had scratched its head upon and damaged.

We finished late, drove home
through the half-dark.
The sky above the braehead
was black-alive with birds -
wheeling, plummeting
tumultuously,
brake-diving the fields - loud
with the tumble-screech of the peewits;
the moonlight eerie-skeerie;
Venus luminous,
low over Catlaw,
with a sprinkle of stars
in the cloud-break:
wind puffing the ember-ash
of the day-fade over Forfar;
smoke from hidden farms;
and the bird-cries barely audible,
as we turned down
to where conifers closed in
with a dark viridian hush;
and the road was dunged
with dead rabbits.

Then up and over
through a wriggle of S-bends,
and we saw the towns of Angus
illuminated
with a trembling touch-type
of fiery dots,
in the lap of the land,
in the let of the valley,
the long and fertile
body of Strathmore.

3. Reminiscence

I

He would study my hands.
They were soft hands. Not
exactly woman's hands, he'd say,
but not workman's hands either;
which worried him
with regard to a secure future
that would keep the wolf from the door.

Second-best, after the no-go of a trade,
was a job with the Milk Marketing Board,
and the possibility of cream;
but I demurred,
nourishing ambitions
of a more artistic nature.

He knew, of course,
that the wolf has sharp and hungry teeth;
that its kin are worldwide;
all equally voracious,
and attacking from every angle.

II

(His own dad had been a dour old devil
at the best of times. Work was manual

if it was man's work, had merit
enough to claim the name of it.

Graft. Guilt. Guilelessness. Low-ceilinged
weaver's cottages, governed

with a kailpot efficiency;
black-leaded, spotless, by courtesy

of Granny's elbow.) Thus, he learned
how not to get his fingers burnt,

played strathspeys, reels and jigs for fun,
before being packed off with a gun.

Now, saddled with the post-war baby,
art was less than even 'maybe'.

With everything seen through the scar
left by the Second World War.

A viewpoint from the deep ditch,
where red ants squeezed through every stitch,

and enemy aircraft raked the road
ahead, with bullets as they bombed

the Burmese dawn from out of the sun.
 I walked along with a balloon,

at five years old, was photographed
in the town-square, holding his hand

while half the world counted its dead,
and half a loaf was little bread.

4. Interlude

'Aye, it's a bonny tune, no question of it.
And a fine singer. He can fairly hold
onto the long notes. And not a voice that wheeps
like a whistling-kettle, either, at the higher pitch.
A treat to listen to. The record's a bit scratched.

A damned disgrace the way some people treat
their musical heritage! A pity, too,
it was in the original Gaelic. I admit
I didna understand a word of it.
You'd want a ... one of those impertinators

to winkle out the sense.'
                              'Impertinator!
And search the world you'd need, for, havers, man,
there's no such thing! You mean "interpreter".
 Where do you get these daft-like mixtures from?
Now, let's give Kenneth McKellar a wee bit spin.

'You'll get the gist of him, I have no doubt!
You'll not be requiring the likes of an impertinator
for Kenneth McKellar, now, will you? Gies a drop
more of the aquavitae. Where's the dumpling?
I canna wait to sink my teeth in it.'

5. Inheritance

In view of an upbringing
among the more basic artefacts,
I made an arse-first,
undignified descent
down from Parnassus:
Parnassus, that is,
in the classical, Grecian sense,
lofty and the like, with no nonsense
from the tradesman's entrance,
where it's barely literate,
and some bastard keeps dropping dog-ends.

To each his own inheritance!

In place of Apollo - an apple or a polo.

In place of the first muse - a blowlamp's blue delirium.

In place of the second muse - the torch-song of a job well
done.

In place of the third muse - a hot bath to wash away the
dirt.

In place of the fourth muse - the washed-away dirt.

In place of Venus - a virus.

In place of the fifth, sixth, and seventh muses,
a carry-out of odds and sods

to the replacement area of the eighth muse - a jubilee
   clip joint.

In place of the ninth muse - bugger-all!

And in case of emergency - a quick telephone call,
reversing the charges,
for a word in your ear from Ogma,

alive, though less than kicking,
in the Celtic darkness:

or, alternatively, push back towards the high ground,
keeping, this time, to the home country -

Schiehallion; Lochnagar; Catlaw;

the hard-bitten, crag-high, scree-slippery, wind-thrummed,
rain-lashed, star-smitten, summit-ridge of the Cuillin.

6. Vision

Plover-light, with an oyster-sheen
in the western sky; seaweed; flat-fish;
jelly-fish; lug-worm casts;
shells; and an inch of tidal-water,
warm, around our bare toes.

At low tide, the islands are linked
by a stretch of sand, walkable-over,
or bumpable-across in a tractor-trailer.
Afterwards, there is a hard track to the farm,
and the old priory, twelfth century,

dedicated to Saint Columba,
who came and left by reason of the skyline.
Gravestones. Decorated slabs. A pile of bones
from a charnel-house. Ruins
sensitively restored where attrition

had worn them to a weary look.
A great Celtic cross dominates
this place of curiosity and pilgrimage.
Some old buildings, converted to holiday-cottages,
are let out at exorbitant rates.

To come here is to step back in time,
with little but the sheep and hoodie-crows
to keep you company, seals wailing unearthly
on the inshore skerries, as you imbibe
an intoxicant sense of the past,

of religious fervour, deprivation,
skill in stonework and design,
dark corners, and the shock of luxuriant flowers,
buttressed against the sea-wind
by lengths of reinforced lattice.

Older yet, on the island,
are the Viking burial-sites
among the sand-dunes;

and even older, the mesolithic shell-mounds -
kitchen-middens pre-dating history.

The tide turns. Crossing back
over the sand, is to step back again
into a time which, according
to scientific thinking, will have laid
the foundations of a launching-pad

for a cybernetic future; the domination
of Earth, by post-biological beings;
an establishment of high I.Qs embarking
on a technological odyssey,
which precognition would have knocked the feet

from Saint Columba, then, and had him kneel
with a hot prayer for that black hole
of no-man's land. A weird inheritance
has staked its pitch
on our graves and the graves of our fathers.

7. The Descent

To look at him you'd think it a wonder
he didn't fall down flat upon his face,
right there and then. He was just skin and bones;
a kind of grim, Duchamp-like figure
in terminal descent; or the critical
domino in a toppling sequence,
too fast for the eye to follow, always
that much further down the line, that much
closer to the anti-climax; though
still able to feed himself, and to keep clean.

He chose delusion rather than defeat.
Stubborn-stupid! Once, with scarcely power
to produce more than a peep from his trumpet,
he padded off outdoors on Christmas Eve,
and played 'Silent Night', still trying to prove
that he was up to it. Meanwhile, the frost
worked upwards from our toes, and did its best
to freeze us to the spot, as we listened
embarrassed, bored, teeth chattering,
under a sky with an all-over star-pattern
of brittle clarity, a haloed moon.

'That wasn't bad', he said, 'not bad at all',
kidding himself; then going back inside
to get his breath back, huddling at the fire,
as though there was no getting close enough
to warm him through. There was but cold comfort
in that post-Calvanist, neo-pictish nook
of the north-east, at that time of the year,
for someone on his last legs. Not much cheer.

8. Elegy

Death is a dirty trick that does not care.
A jersey on the sofa-back, a hair,
the tang of after-shave in the bathroom,
remain for hours or days, but not for long.
He was skinny as a rake, at last; though strong
enough to be frustrating to the tomb.

The winter saw him off. He'd gone outside
without his hat in terminal ice-cold.
A step too far. The problem was a chronic
disorder of the lungs. The doctor blamed
the bloody cigarettes, the Woodbines; claimed
that down the years had tarred his lungs up thick.

My father had his own theory, and would
have none of the smoking nonsense. He had
blown his trumpet once too often. The
breath-control required in passages
of trumpet-solos, weakened him by stages,
so he maintained, the price of artistry.

I travelled north on the day-train, two days
before the funeral. A sunlit haze
glamourised the town. I dreaded that last look,
the traditional parting that is far too late
and too much for the likes of me, that state
of stony otherworldliness. I took

no more than a passing glance. The day
was fading to a velvet hush. He lay
among whispers, varnished pine. I thought
of him hunkering down over a burst pipe,
or installing a new toilet, the type
you bring the next-door neighbours in to look at.

He'd left a bottle half-full of whisky
on the kitchen-shelf. The sky, that night, was frosty.
The stars came up like sparks from off a spade.
I wear his coat yet. There was thirteen pounds
inside his wallet. Next morning, the birds,
waited, as usual, for the bread he scattered.

The Flaying of Marsyas

Robin Robertson

nec quicquam nisi vulnus erat (Ovid, Metamorphoses,
VI, 288)

I

A bright clearing. Sun among the leaves,
sifting down to dapple the soft ground, and rest
a gilded bar against the muted flanks of trees.
In the flittering green light the glade
listens in and breathes.

A wooden pail; some pegs, a coil of wire;
a bundle of steel flensing knives.

Spread-eagled between two pines,
hooked at each hoof to the higher branches,
tied to the root by the hands, flagged
as his own white cross,
the satyr Marsyas hangs.

Three stand as honour guard:
two apprentices, one butcher.

II

Let's have a look at you, then.
Bit scrawny for a satyr,
all skin and whipcord, is it?
Soon find out.
So, think you can turn up with your stag-bones
and outplay Lord Apollo?
This'll learn you. Fleece the fucker.
Sternum to groin.
Tickle does it? Fucking bastard,
coming down here with your dirty ways...
Armpit to wrist, both sides.

Chasing our women...
Fine cuts round hoof and hand and neck.
Can't even speak the language proper.
Transverse from umbilicus to iliac crest,
half-circling the waist.
Jesus. You fucking stink, you do.
Hock to groin, groin to hock.
That's your inside leg done:
no more rutting for you, cunt.

Now. One of you on each side.
Blade along the bone, find the tendon,
nick it and peel, nice and slow.
A bit of shirt-lifting, now, to purge him,
pull his wool over his eyes
and show him Lord Apollo's rapture;
pelt on one tree, him on another:
the inner man revealed.

III

Red Marsyas. Marsyas écorché,
splayed, shucked of his skin
in a tug and rift of tissue;
his birthday suit sloughed
the way a sodden overcoat is eased
off the shoulders and dumped.
All memories of a carnal life
lifted like a bad tattoo,
live bark from the vascular tree:
raw Marsyas unsheathed.

Or dragged from his own wreckage
dressed in red ropes
that plait and twine his trunk
and limbs into true definition,
he assumes the flexed pose of the hero:
the straps and buckles of ligament
glisten and tick on the sculpture
of Marsyas, muscle-man.
Mr Universe displays the map of his body:

the bulbs of high ground carved
by the curve of gully and canal,
the tributaries tight as ivy or the livid vine,
and everywhere, the purling flux of blood
in the land and the swirl of it flooding away.

Or this: the shambles of Marsyas,
the dark chest meat marbled with yellow fat,
his heart like an animal breathing
in its milky envelope,
the viscera a well-packed suitcase
of chitterlings and palpitating tripe.
A man dismantled, a tatterdemalion
torn to steak and rind,
a disappointing pentimento
or the toy that can't be reassembled
by the boy Apollo, raptor, vivisector.
The sail of stretched skin thrills and snaps
in the same breeze that makes his nerves
fire, his bare lungs scream.
Stripped of himself and from his twin:
the stiffening scab and the sticky wound.
Marsyas the martyr, a god's fetish,
hangs from the tree like bad fruit.

The Funerals

Gordon Mason

Three polished limousines slide up the Shankill past
H. Stevenson, the green-grocer, Jackie Phillips and Sons,
Then past the bombed-out wallpaper shop's remains.

Each car is led, tail-coat, top-hat,
By one of the undertaker's three professional men
Spectacled, self-important, out-of-step.

Among the affairs of this mid-afternoon -
What remains of them, three ordinary folk
Bombed off the floor they stood on, one

Postage-stamped to the door, now passing by
As if they had been far away and here
Returning home with the answer they can't give

To the question everyone asks.
Outside their deaths an English soldier
Peers from a doorway just in case the truth

Breaks cover from beneath its canopy of flowers
And breaks the terrible silence of the afternoon.
Better for all of us the dead are underground.

There is no sound though but the limousines'
Condensing breath expiring into a cold October air,
That, and the regular tick-tick the mourners'

Rolled umbrellas make against the street like
Mine-detectors hovering just above the ground
That point and say, this way, this way.

The Gecko

Jeffrey Turner

High up and chancing on such a pause
in the slope of the land, a level
smooth and still as a pool
caught in a shrug of the mountain, you feel
maybe you ought to tread more carefully,

pretending trespass on the remains perhaps
of some unreasonable significance;
just missing an explanation by a footstep.
But the donkey's already gone
that has at last sawn through

a worthless voice and, transformed,
escaped among the twisted wire-like stems
of the olive trees,
at an end with patient attendance,
a dropping left as an adieu

and all there is to tell what happened.
Elsewhere the island will show the few
stray bullets of history it has stopped.
The rest is hearsay; of the gods
and heroes and their disturbances

a handful of shaky clues, washed ashore
to cultivate a refuge, green
with possibilities. As shadows uncrumple
to cool the air with night, a storm
flickers behind us and the hills

like headlamps on the track,
hunting the doublings of the terraced road.
We cannot avoid the olives as we walk.
They squash like beetles underfoot
and stick to shoes like melting tar.

The fireflies' small courtesies of light
drift across our path. Deep to our right,
where the lemon grove must be,
they plot the moist air above the stream,
playing with switches in countless

imaginary rooms, where nothing
is beyond belief.
In this liquorice darkness
each is a brightness
that sees no further than itself,

and we believe in the persuasive
fascination of their astrology,
their intimate constellations,
though trusting less and less
as we move toward that stranger island

where names are no more
than these syllables of light
and we shall be again the sole
inhabitants with only secrets,
like the guessed-at trees, between us.

The balcony floats,
a lungful of light, on the cicadas'
geometric rhythms and the gurgling of scooters.
A dog barks and barks at nothing it can see.
And when the lights are out

the mosquito's whine will find a way
to end in blood. The sounds rise like colours
scratching through the black as we sit, stumped
over postcards that expect no answer.
Moths, illustrious and plain-knitted,

stub themselves against the lamp, their hectic,
impatient wings erasure marks on the light's
opened page, settling for this ersatz moon,
a treasury of dead insects,
three feet above our heads.

And tonight the gecko chooses to come
to feed its noiselessness on these flakes
of silence; a wraith-like form,
weak tea-coloured, as though
on such a diet, accumulating like dust, it might

in time spirit itself away, replete.
On the wall, head down, its body signed off
by the tail's careful flourish, it waits,
a calm and dangerous island.
The black beacons of its eyes illuminate

the furling sails gathering round the low,
confident profile that does not waver
as it prepares for each abrupt coincidence,
in no hurry until it pounces, and another moth
is posted to the gecko's dark interior.

Imaginary Furniture

Adèle Geras

He said: Keep them still.
Don't let them flap about so.
She concluded that her hands were birds.

She was too far
from any sea for seagulls.
Why did she wake to cries;
scavenging for rubbish in her ears?

The bed has white sheets like icing.
Movement, any wind, blows
blue peaks, sad hollows into the fabric:
a soft frosting teased into points
with silver forks.

Sails, in a procession of pale triangles
roll along the thread of the horizon.

Suspicions like small hedgehogs
nudge her flesh. Also petals
from a wrinkled flower, also words
that are soundless, but feel
like broken crockery.

Keep your hands in your lap.
Only foreigners wave their hands about,
he says, and she has white birds
growing from each wrist
in a vibration of thin feathers.

The order of the bracelets on her arm
matters.
She wears them all the time
in this
(silver, wood, ivory, amber, plastic)

order, and removes them
for washing up, and bathing and at night.
They hurt if she leans on them,
so for writing she builds a tower in this
(silver, wood, ivory, amber, plastic)
order, somewhere where she can see them.

When her daughter hears bracelets
slide and click and slide in empty rooms,
she says: Mother.
My mother is coming.

Everyone has forgotten how to eat.
The tablecloth is mountainous terrain
and all the guests are crooning to their feet.
Everyone has forgotten how to eat.
No one has come she thought she'd like to meet.
Her crochet is unravelling again.
Everyone has forgotten how to eat.
The tablecloth is mountainous terrain.

Someone has been flyposting the wall behind her eyes:

(Jilani's Alankar Discount Stores Access via
ramp LikkerPikker Dido Pizza eat in or take
 away Sangam Paradise Phonecard Internatio
Claremont Friendship I Chuni's Saree Palace
 Day-old bread Clarence in pieces in Willow)

and when she opens them, neon lights go on and off
    pink-blink blink-pink
        Welcome to the billboard.

Headless polystyrene shapes
understudying necks, are hung with necklaces
of gold too yellow by half.

Hands up anyone who still believes in glitter.

dance on deckchairs
paint cold lunches
puncture Care Bears
knit your hunches
patch your mother
peel your fishes
slice your brother
dice your wishes

This is what she keeps
in her dresser drawers:

twenty-seven lime green cats.
Silly women hanging upside down
with flowers where their hair should be.
A chair (over which someone
has poured a sheet) under a parasol.
Two sisters. One old man
wearing brocade, pleased with his own beard.
A teacup, fragile as bones,
centred in the full moon of a saucer.
Ballet shoes: blood-spotted, satin.
A calendar. A theatre full of knives.

Plates stare at her
from the dresser shelves.
If only *her* face
were sprigged with blossom,
bows, or ivy garlands,
streaked with royal blue
or peach, or yesterday's best green.

If no one is looking,
jugs bow to her
and she curtseys. Dishes
in the dark
exchange short
brittle sentences,
crazed promises,
fractured sighs.

On Mondays, he allows her to explore
the garden and the shops. To hesitate

would mean another fortnight on the floor
which she keeps swept and clean: immaculate.

Every third Tuesday, they rehearse a war
with weapons she finds hard to contemplate.

On Wednesdays, she may stand beside the door
and fret and shiver, but not speculate

about the ashes which she can't ignore
and which appear each Thursday, violate

tiles and linoleum. And even more
she fears that somebody will allocate

biscuits on Friday, as they did before.
These matters are a chore to regulate.

On Saturday, her hand becomes a claw,
a splendid tool to dig with. It's too late

by Sunday to adjust a whole week's score.
She has no time left to reciprocate.

In the High Atlas

Andrew Greig

Dawn - cold - we stumbled through
faults in the plateau, boots shot,
lips split, our stubborn mule
the only optimist left
as we slid and clattered
down that gully ...

But halfway in, the ravine shrugged
or the mule changed its mind
the way history does once in a while:

    a slash across the hillside
    glittered like a blade
    below it everything

        bled

Green

The mule shucked our baggage and ran.

***

Five faces, four human, one
more or less,
nose down in that water.

Drank. Threw up. Drank more.
Lay belly-down by cool waters.

    'Un source,' Ken murmured,
    'sprung straight from the dust,
    doubtless a glacier melt
    sent down to us
        by high powers.
    This dawn is not my enemy's.'

49

Water in our eyes, ears, hair,
we stared at the terraces below
stacked like plates, each
with its garnish:
almond in blossom, olives, figs,
and the morning breeze
like a perfect waiter
                                      shimmied up
to ask what we most wanted...

Between aridity and life
    runs a slash
the width of an irrigation channel -
    miracle, for sure
but one honed by human hands.

    'Juxta
              position,'
    said Stella as she
rinsed her hair from red to fair,
knocked out her hat and spat,
'the whole armature of experience,
the motor of modern art.
        If I had a hammer
I'd knock up a sestina.'

'No, no!' we cried.
    She lay back, cracked her pursed lips,
        began to whistle.

    'Sod that,' Brock said, hoisted
the jewelled binoculars that hung
from the neck of the mule:
    'Woodsmoke, a village, water-mills,
    five hours hence. Ya beauty!
                        - Let's roll.'

⁕

50

Up front she sang,
'These Boots are Made for Walking'.
Behind her, Kenny ducked and hummed,
'Dark Isle' and 'The Flowers of the Forest'.
She turned and looked at him
and between them flew something
like a pass
                so quick I couldn't tell
who now held the ball,

but something had been exchanged
and happiness was punted
way into the sky
where it hung for hours
descending slowly at dusk
as we entered the village.

***

Three weeks into the High Atlas
we could only guess the argument.
Hard light, harsh land, honed faces
with manners more courteous than ours
and a knife winking on the hip
and hospitality proportional to poverty
as is the way
with mountain people in this world
as though their scabby villages
are last undrowned fragments
of a clearer world...

    You won't like this thought,
but there was a war on
in a not so distant desert
and we wondered
whether chaos, like cruelty,
is a constant
that changes only its location
and so will always find a home.

I said you wouldn't like it.

***

We have gone behind the war,
Ken whispered,
as though it were a curtain, a
        tapestry of violence,
and now the heart draws back,
        revealing -

   A mule clicked down the canyon.
On it an old and humble man
relaxed, radio cradled to his ear.

'Labesse! Becher! How goes the war?'

   'As always. Did you meet my son
   at the souk - has he sold goats?
   These damn Yankee batteries, so dear...'

We sheltered in the shadow of the reddish rocks.
The war went on through tiny speakers,
distorted, lost in that high stoney place,
awful of course
        but not everything
for we had glimpsed the timeless villages
and now shared oranges and cigarettes with him.

Dry smoke, sharp juice -

all life was in   the alteration
desert war   rest in the mountains
head-splitting heat   cool under the rock
silent afternoon   sputtering radio
this orange   this cigarette
desire   the end of desire
this Berber   these Christians

   and like a knife from its sheath,
   like a foot from its boot,
   came a slight easing...

'Now tourists don't come to the city,
the shops don't buy from us
when they can't sell to them, and thus
we can't buy feed for our dry season.
Sheep and goats starve alike.
Vous savez, tourists like some birds
are signs of peace and settled weather.

O send down clouds, Allah!
If we can't have peace or tourism,
let us at least have rain.
And if you have no money, friends,
then give us a song.'

We looked to Brock, he shook his head.
'My mind is on my ain countree,
where clouds like grizzlin bairns
hang girning on the mountain's side.'

Stella coughed and then
with unaccustomed shyness rose.
'An old lament,' she said then sang
in her husky thin high voice:

'Love is mostly dejection,
We were drunk on projection.
But now I'm quite sober,
And I'm in my right mind -

But I never loved no one
Like I loved that someone
And I saw this world most clearly
When I was going blind...'

She stopped and stooped a moment
against the red sky, bitter-sweet
Heartbreak adjusting her sandal.

The Hadji clapped slowly, twice.
'Though you have food, I see you're hungry.
You have water, yet you thirst.

53

I do not know your pilgrimage
but I invite you to follow
me back to our village.'

He rose and touched his hand
first to his lips, then to his heart
and we in clumsy fashion responded.
He remounted and led us there,
poor, assured, a distant war
cradled to his ear.

In the highest village

'No,' we said gently, 'we do not want
to come and see you "make the folklore",
no, nor take pictures of your daughters
miming prettily in the fields.
These travesties are painful, and must cease.'

'Wakha,' the old man grinned, stroked
his lang neb. 'Agreed.
So let's sit till the yellow rider
slips from the saddle of the sky.
(I'm expected to speak this way,
don't let it charm or bother you.)'

We sat down by a broken wall
around a few untended trees
in thin dry grass like clumps of hair
clung to an aged skull.
'Peaceful here, we like it.'

'You've noticed, but are too polite to say.
The terraces of the old ones are crumbling.
In empty palmeries the water channels
return to sand.
                    Now nothing here
holds water long, the land returns
to slow mode, half asleep, unkempt
where once were dates and almonds,
saffron, olives, wheat gleaned by goats.'

'My country too has empty hillsides,
old walls crumbling by the sea.'

 'We did not call it "folklore" then.
 We called it nothing but our way.
 Our festivals were enacted
 for no eyes but our own.
 There was no talk of "the community".'

'There was a cow, chickens, a bit land,
a boat dragged high upon the machar.
Their houses too were small and dark,
full of smoke thick and familiar
as fatigue and dignity. Doubtless
their eyes watered.'

 'My friend, I see you too
 have a peasant's mentality.
 Your hands, broad and coarse as mine,
 suggest you could work leather
     or the fields.'

I can take a hint. What needs done?'

 'Shokaran. This wall must be rebuilt
 against the goats. Also some hoeing,
 the highest channel shored again.
 May I allot your muscular friend,
 yourself, the unmarried woman,
    each to their suited task?
 Your patient mule
 can walk in circles, drawing water.'

'Pal: you're on.'

***

(That pointy ball of happiness you caught
and snuck into your pack when you were searching,
long ways from home, and lost, and found again,
together with a handshake and an honest trade
and eyes met for once across the barriers -

be close now as remembered hills,
the Alt a' Mhuilann, and Rest and Be Thankful.)

Cheap Labour

We spent the war in that high corrie
beyond all roads and radio,
worked long days for Hadji,
dossed down nights inside his byre,
worked hard, slept well,
content to shape another's garden.

'Sometimes salvation,
like a worthy ox,
cannot be yoked head-on',
the old man grinned.
'Anyway, you're cheap labour
while our young men are in the city
or baking bread on the plains of war.'

And Stella borrowed my penknife
to scratch above the old man's mantle

Sweat and sleep and in-between
smoke and watch the moon awhile
flattering the scraggy palms;
may channeled water flow each day
and be clear discourse in your dreams.

***

Days of Sweat and Succour

　　Brock took up the filthy oud
our gaffer handed him one night,
found it took his crippled fingers well.
Fast by an ingle, night by night
he acquired the music of the gnawa
that can drive out devils
or drive insane.

And Stella started to relax among the men.
Women walked a little taller when she passed,
and showed her how to rim her eyes with kohl.
And Stella said,
　　　'All truth is good news
　　　how dark it seems'

And, later,
　　　Happiness
　　　is not my happiness,
And she wrote little
but her hands were steady.

Ken's hands grew harder as he worked
salvaging clapped-out machinery,
but his mind moved less like metal,
more like water: he said,

　　'We got it wrong.
　　The world is everything
　　outside the text. Man,
　　it's so mean to always mean!'

And, after long days working
the two-man saw among the pines,

　　'As a working hypothesis
　　it's not entirely ridiculous
　　to live and act as if
　　an Other exists.'

He became
        a favourite of the children
for they found him
not entirely ridiculous
and he could make things disappear
and reappear,
and tie
most complex knots that pulled
free with one tug
on the end produced from his ear.

A Graduation Ceremony

The young men came home.
The war was over
or rather moved elsewhere
and we were fit but surplus.

Our last task:
clearing the village's main well.
Brock abseiled down
and many muffled curses came back up
till finally he surfaced
covered in gunge. He silently
gave the Hadji
an ancient sack that clunked,
then plodded off to wash.
The bucket went down,
came up clear.
                'Well done,'
Hadji said quietly, 'and now
it's time to say farewell.
You have connected East to West
with honest sweat, now you must go
back to your people. But first
come to the square for a feast tonight.'

    We washed, changed to travelling clothes,
and walked under stars
we'd never see so clear again
to the meeting place among the palms.

The Hadji clapped his hands
and the farewell feast began.
We smoked and shot the breeze till dawn,
much singing, Brock played
most furious for the dancers,
great bullshit among the ox-turds.
Firelight rising, and a touch of opium
sticky on our words until
 the worlds began to slide again
  the first cock stirred
   and we were
    in for

    Another change of scene.

Brock kept the oud but
wrapped his ancient leather jacket
round the wildest child there.

 The Immam gave Ken a chased leather belt
 slipped through the loop of the Koran,
 buckled tight. 'Don't dispute this, friend,'

  Stella hummed and coughed
  as though about to make a speech
  but only held her palm out to the people
  then slowly placed it on her heart
  and turned away

and we left that village
one star awake.

In Memory of Vincent Cox

born Lambeth 1923, died Harpenden January 1991

Nick Drake

for Iain Cox

Who loved the knack of luck, of stakes and odds,
an ace, seven sevens, a hole in one;

who disappeared on Saturday afternoons
through the forbidden ribbon door

of the obscure betting shop, to reappear
later in his old leather armchair

smiling his winnings, smoking, drinking tea
by the potful, and watching the tv -

Who loved to fly, Lancasters, a bomber's moon
on midnight raids, on Dresden in '45,

the figurine homes, churches, the platz and parks
razed, each family walking shades

where china turned to ash, and tears to salt,
glass buckled, light went blind, the phosphorus heart

crazed; who still came home against the odds
in a plane he called *Mizpah* ('in God we Trust').

Who traded his wings in post-war civvy street
for wife and son, the suburbs, a salesman's car

and business travelling north to Staffordshire's
bleak pottery furnaces and crucibles;

who loved the lucent angles and singing rim
of cut-glass fluted from a bulb of light

on the blowing rod; sand, potash, lime,
oxides and carbonates, transfigured to

an affluence of decanters and services,
pastoral figures on the mantlepiece,

an attic of first editions packed in straw
for his after-life; and two porcelain

lucky angels cool in his left hand
as the right turned aces up or cast the dice.

Who watched with us on winter afternoons
the Sunday war film, equally black and white;

clipped, self-effacing, nonchalant braveries,
one engine spluttering, impossibly

homing on a last wing and a prayer
to the orchestra's finale and dawn's light.

Who crash-landed in his armchair, years later,
the guilty survivor when his wife passed on

to where neither luck nor prayer could win her back;
whose photograph would never speak, however

long he stared, sat in the early dark
among unwashed tea cups and full ash-trays,

in the slow day's silent games of Patience.
Who carefully washed the cups, put them away

and tidied his house; who wrote a pencilled note
on the back of an envelope; unanswerable

loss, bad years revenged, self-punishment;
still why, by nail and noose and rope, did he

bail out of the attic's small trap door
into the hall's frosted January light?

Who played the joker, but who was not this;
the undertaker's mistaken parting

running through his hair on the wrong side;
a cotton smile on his face as if he might

rise to greet us, Lazarus at his wake,
who still believes himself to be blessed by luck.

Who I last remember as a window ghost
in his living room reflected in the night

on an incandescent lawn of frost
ironing his white shirts in an empty room.

Who his elder brother recalled in a better story;
White City dog-track, winter '33;

mother, the infamous gambler who seems
to have wagered and lost her husband in a bet,

was having no run of luck, but staked her last
(her return tube fare) in a four-dog race

on the outside track; gates up, the inside three
collide and knock each other cold and out,

while Outside Chance raced on under the lights
to an illuminated victory

at hopeless-to-one; which brought for Wally and Vince
a slap-up tea and a taxi home to bed.

Who was released out of a winter day,
his secrets, wishes and excuses turned to ash

while we stood in his absence, uncertain
tick-tack men signing *goodbye, goodbye*

to a lucky man who seemed to lose himself,
his gentle laughter; a chancer of odds

grounded, who loved to fly, the navigator
over enemy country, charts and compasses,

flight angles, lucky angels, blessed wings,
seeking the constant, simple, bright North Star

in the winter sky he knew by heart.
Iain, now I remember how we'd play

for coppers or matchsticks when we were kids,
your father deftly shuffling the pack;

who might forgive - with the grace of his good luck,
with the ghost of a chance - these words as my low stake

raised against loss and in his memory,
though I can find no words to say to you.

Lingua

Stephen Duncan

Neither spoke the other's tongue
but assumed English
for the practicalities of their life:

those squared-off elements
like soap, 'a pound of ...'
and the insistent letters from his bank.

Naked, he was invisible,
dumb, until he donned
a heavy dressing gown,

flicking water from his hair
as he murmured a line
from a *cacciatore's* song.

To tease her or in temper
he might reveal the impulse
of his mother-tongue,

chuckling as he slipped
an allegro *con fuoco*
inside her throat-furred Russian.

Their intimacy was in French -
in letters both billet-doux
and plain speaking when they separated,

or met in her bed,
the scented middle room of their flat
where she plucked the curling hairs

of imperfect brows,
shearing graves and acutes
with her Moscow tone.

She crooned to him,
retaining her underwear
at his request.

Listening to a Russian Choir

Vern Rutsala

The voices sing
   of long avenues
      inside stones,
of distances so
   vast you've
      run out of miles
to count them with.
   The voices say follow
     if you can
keep up, stay warm,
   our winter has no end.
      Forget all those
hours lost with
   your cold hands
     folded, obeying some
teacher's bilious frown.
   We promise you'll never
     have to color between
the lines again
   or ask permission
     to leave a room.
So scribble your
   straight and narrow
     fat and crooked -
we couldn't care less.
   Let parts of speech
     change places like
partners at a dance -
   choose St Vitus
     if you want - he's good.
These songs mean
   business. They plant
     the itch to fly
deep in your shoulders,
   hint at your latent talent
     for wings and love

66

to slip the noose
          of language, letting
                    nouns and verbs
disagree whenever they
          like, begging commas
                    to swim off like manic
tadpoles. The voices
          rise and fall, tease,
                    caress. They keen
all edges smooth, they rough up
                    your pantywaist
nostalgia just for
          fun or swarm like
                    fire looping up
a flue, then swirl
          with the spit and hiss
                    of downed wires
spilling their sap.
          Keep up if you can,
                    stay warm, the journey
is no longer than our
          winter that has no end.
                    See the cathedrals
we build so easily
          with our music, see
                    how easily we topple
them like children's
          blocks. We can build
                    more any time we please.
These songs won't
          let you add up
                    your life's days
with the dull sonnets
          of cashier's slips -
                    they know the toothache
in the hearts of lettuce,
          the tragic lives
                    of artichokes,
the dark insomnia
          of potatoes
                    and semolina's migraines.

But pay no attention -
                make bouquets of all
                        your loose ends
and mail them
                to the sandman -
                        you have no more
need for sleep,
                that abandoned factory.
                        Forget the backing and filling
of dependent clauses,
                let the periodic
                        sentence die of natural
causes. They say dive off
                the deep end, let
                        your dry wit drown
and free yourself
                of the tyranny of keys
                        and better mousetraps.
We know a secret
                inoculation against
                        the law of gravity
and we'll make damn sure
                all your enemies' boats
                        pound to kindling
on the rocks - this is only
                one of many fringe benefits.
                        So fly with us and call
all the Milky Way's
                unlisted numbers
                        one by one
while soaring in our
                troika and throwing
                        caviar to the wolves.

Manhunt

Rebecca Hayes

Months it took to find him, stalking our prey
at gatherings of squawking friends: someone
standing quietly, who didn't belong,
a stranger at a party, a new face
in the busy pub, someone on the edge
whom no one really knew, and wouldn't miss.

Some I followed home, watching how they moved
around their territory, checking their hours,
their tastes and habits. Others I tracked down
office corridors, to name-plates on doors,
telephone voices heard in rooms; I brushed
past them in the lift, offering a smile.

I tried out chance encounters in the street,
searching for the right face, the eager look
that showed intelligence, the body borne
with easy confidence, a hint of good.
None was what we wanted: all had that faint
quiver betraying pride, those tell-tale lips.

Then a gentle voice heard across a room
when I wasn't listening: I saw him caught
in sunlight by a window, a forest
of people standing between; like a doe
grazing in a clearing, he must have sensed
me there, meeting my eyes as I moved in.

Flooding the ceiling, moonlight made a pool
I floated from that night, a mirror where
I saw him moving on me, his bare back
and white globes of buttocks, his mane my hands
were raking. Out of my body, high as
a hawk, I watched my quarry wait for me
to fall down like a spider on its thread.
We lay there heavy in eah other's arms,

and when he felt me breathing evenly,
he slipped away. The night he disappeared
it was as if I'd eaten him alive,
he'd gone completely. You were there instead.

Men

Kate Clanchy

I like the simple sort, the soft white collared ones
smelling of wash that someone else has done,
of apples, hard new wood. I like the thin-skinned,
outdoor, crinkled kind, the athletes, big-limbed,
who stoop to hear, the moneyed men, the unironic
leisured sort who balk at jokes and have to blink,
the men with houses, kids in cars, who own
the earth and love it, know themselves at home
here, and so don't know they're born, or why
born is hard, but snatch life smack from the sky,
a cricket ball caught clean that fills the hand.
I put them all at sea. They peer at my dark land
as if through sun on dazzling waves, and laugh.

Mount Pleasant

Angela Inglis

My grandmother saved her life
for the future,
and for heaven.

Her house hung sideways
on a hill
smelling of mildew
silence
and the dead.

And yet each day
she dressed for them.
At night she called out
at their doors
talking to their ghosts.

Sitting by the iron range,
she wrote letters in the semi-dark
to her sisters in Africa and America,
detailing the minutiae of her daily round,
her neat and careful copperplate
moving like a knot
strangling any
piece of space.

I am talking of a heroine.
She made something of a nothing life.

When I opened up
my grandmother's old pantry
I found her dinner set
put there for some indefinite day;
and as I pulled the white
and deep blue plates
out of the dark
they fell apart.

No Hands

Vicki Feaver

When all the water had run from her mouth,
and I'd rubbed her arms and legs,
and chest and belly and back,
with clumps of dried moss;
and I'd put her to sleep in a nest of grass,
and spread her dripping clothes on a bush,
and held her again - her heat passing
into my breast and shoulder,
the breath I couldn't believe in
like a tickling feather on my neck,
I let myself cry. I cried for my hands
my father cut off; for the lumpy itching scars
of my stumps; for the silver hands -
my husband gave me - that spun and wove
but had no feeling; and for my handless arms
that let my baby drop - unwinding
from the tight swaddling-cloth
as I drank from the brimming river.
And I cried for my hands that sprouted
in the red-orange mud - the hands
that write this, grasping
her curled fists.

In Grimm's telling of this story the woman's hands
grow back because she has been good for seven years.
But in a Russian version her hands grow as she plunges
her arms into a river to save her drowning baby.

Old People

Christina Dunhill

Wet mouths in dark rooms, old people wait
for a kiss, for a mole on a cheek
to brush your cheek, for you to fall
over their feet splayed out in ancient slippers,
their thick, brown-stockinged, knobbled legs.
Low in overblown floral chairs, they sit
with their enormous khaki handkerchiefs,
dabbing at something.

Old people: they live alone, their green bakelite clocks
tick loud through anything you say, you can't ignore
the patterns of their walls, that tyranny of roses
marching your eye on a meaningless pilgrimage,
again and again and again. They drink brown drinks
from glasses filmy as their eyes; they want you to hold
                                               them,
their hands are ready, loose skin, brown spots,
the slippery veins.

There's always a ball of wool coming from them,
they knit and knit and knit, do darning with mushrooms,
embroider cushions, put smocking on dresses;
they cry in chairs. They leave themselves about in
                                            pieces -
three pairs of glasses, three hard snappy cases,
mugs of livid gums with teeth - you look for things
you half expect to find and know you shouldn't;
you don't know what stays in.

Old people want you to hold them together.
They lie in bed and smile and watch
your shaking fingers plait their hair.

Post-War Almanac

Clare MacDonald Shaw

As prophesied
after the long war -

years of shooting stars -
a change of weather.

To appease the new god
bronze images were melted,

days axed from the week.
A sign came:

oil rose through water,
blackening the shore.

Let out again, the sun
deposited its gold.

Brittle with drought,
the map split,

tilting houses off the earth.
Livestock at market

panicked, leapt fences;
the seed grew sour.

Swollen with air,
the hungry run to St Luck's.

Her gospel is written in light,
moving green oracles.

This day is her feast;
her chapel's stacked

with paper hearts,
the valentines of prayer.

Tinfoil, plaster,
she's drawn through the streets;

her banner's an eye
sewn up with gilt thread.

Suitors ride the floats
pricking gut balloons;

for those who fall
under the covered wheels

she does not intercede.

A Private Bottling

Don Paterson

Back in the front room that, an hour before
we led, lamp by lamp, into the darkness,
I sit down, turn the radio on low
as the last girl on the planet still awake
reads a dedication to the ships
and puts on a recording of the ocean.
I have evenly spaced out a chain of nips
in a big fairy-ring, in every glass
the tincture of a failed geography,
its dwindling burns and forests, whin-fires, heather,
the sklent of its wind and its salty rain,
the love-worn habits of its working folk,
their speech, and by imaginative extension
how they sing, make love, or tell a joke.
So I have a good nose for this sort of thing.
I will take each fierce kiss smack on the lips
and let their gold tongues slide along my tongue
as each gives up, in turn, its little song
of the patient years in glass and sherryoak,
its shy negotiations with the sea,
the soil, the trick of how the peat-smoke
was locked inside it like a black thought.

Tonight I toast her with the extinct malts
of Ardlussa, Ladyburn and Dalintober
and an ancient pledge of passionate indifference,
ochón ó do dhóigh mé mo chlairseach ar a shon,
over and over and over, till I believe it.
When the circle is closed and I have drunk myself sober
I will tilt the blinds a little, and watch
the dawn grow in a glass of liver salts,
wait for the birds, the milk float's sweet nothings,
then slip back to the bed where she lies curled,
replace her warm ass in my freezing lap
gently, like a live egg in the wrong nest,
as dead to her as she is to the world.

Here we are again; it is precisely
twelve, fifteen or thirty years later,
exactly one turn up the spiral chamber
that is the sum of what I can remember.
Each glass holds its micro-episode
in suspension, till it plays again,
revivified by a suave connoiseurship
that deepens in the silence and the dark
to something like an infinite sensitivity.
This is not romantic conceit; get this - my father
used to know a man who'd taste the sea,
then leave his nets strung out along the bay
because there were no fish in it that day.
Everything is in everything else. It is a matter
of attunement, as once, through the hiss and backwash
I steered the dial into the voice of God
slightly to the left of Hilversum,
almost drowned by some big, blurry waltz
the way Sirius obscured its dwarf companion
for centuries, till someone thought to look.
In this way, I can isolate the feints
of feminine effluvia, carrion, shit,
those rogues and toxins only introduced
to give the composition a little weight
as rough harmonics do the violin-note
or Pluto, Chiron and the lesser saints
might do to our lives, for all you know.
(By God, you would recognise their absence
as anyone would testify, having sank
a glass of *North British*, run off a patent still
in some godforsaken satellite of Edinburgh;
a bleak spirit, no amount of caramel
could sweeten or disguise, its after-effect
somewhere between a blanket bath and a sad wank.
There is, no doubt, a bar in Lothian
where it is sworn upon and swallowed neat
by furloughed riggers and the Special Police,
men who hate the company of women).

O whiskies of Long Island and Provence!
This little number catches at the throat
but is all sweetness in the finish, my palate
counting through burning brake-fluid, nicotine,
pastis, Diorissimo and wet grass.
Here is another, all smiles and lip-service
with a kick like a smacked face in a train station.
Frost, semen, hashish, oblivion. I could go on forever.
A toast, then, since tonight I take the waters
with the more than simply absent: all the friends
we did not make, our faceless ushers, bridesmaids,
our four Shelties, three now ghosts of ghosts;
so here's tae us, wha's like us, damn few
and they're a' deid, or even less than deid,
our douce sons and our lovely loud-mouthed daughters
who will, at this late hour, be fully grown,
perhaps with unborn children of their own.
Don't be fooled; this is never true
feeling, but is sentimental residue.
This time, I will get away Scot-free
and die before her absence touches me.

The Test

Stephanie Bowgett

They took her blood, spun it, spread
it clear as a sweet-paper on glass. It told
the story of a baby, his nodding head
full of sea; a baby with legs that would fold,
and twang anarchic as rubber bands,
a baby with a back-bone open as herring's:
his laugh would froth bubbles, his anenome hands
fan open, wave and close; never hold anything.

They spoke carefully to her,
covered the small hole
with a strip of sticking plaster
on the skin inside her left elbow.
It healed well. All you can see there now
is a trace of a pale blue shadow.

This is just to say why she did not wax poetic

Betsy Robin Schwartz

The deliveries came into the
 kitchen with the sunlight.
First the ice, hauled from the
 wagon and placed in the box.
I took out all the food
 replaced it and rearranged it.
Then the eggs and milk and
 cheese and butter. I smiled
 at the horses then balanced
 the daily dairy through the
 foyer and down the long hall
 then opened the icebox latch
 with my knee (bruise), re-
 arranging, setting these
 perishables in place.
Just in time, I'd gathered
 the scissors and knives
 for the grinder-man's
 whistle.

Before the doctor woke, I had
 gathered all the coins from
 the house money jar and walked
 to the Park Avenue market.
I filled my bags with soaps,
 vinegar, oils, cleansers,
 paper, pen nibs, ink and
 polish; and with just a penny
 or two leftover - the first spare
 change in three years - bought
 myself four small sweet plums
 because I knew the taste of them
 only as a girl.
(I laboured long over the thought
 of purchasing plums, I could

not remember ever buying anything
solely for myself. It seemed a
wicked, wonderful thing to do.)

I did not know the weight of the
bags until I let go of them
near the pantry.
Carefully I unwrapped the plums,
pumped the water to rinse them,
set them in a plain blue bowl,
and placed them between the
cottage cheese and the eggs.
My raw hands prepared the skillet
and the stove, sliced bread,
stirred the cereal, scrambled
eggs and placed his toast on
the table in the dining room.

He was sated and gone before
I sat to nibble on dregs of
spongy eggs.
I dried the last fork, and mixed
the starch for his shirts
placing the picture of perfect
ripe round plums on the empty
slate in my mind; purple and
red pulled taut across lobes of
firm flesh.

I'd hung the laundry (rinsed corsets
and all) and fretted over drying
time in the husky New Jersey
humidity.
The perspiration beaded on my
brow as I pressed his clothes
and thought of the cold dew
that would make the four fruits
glisten like the red wheel-
barrow under the clothesline
in the backyard.

I fed all the chickens except the
  white one which I swung by
  the neck, plucked and prepared
  for dinner.
I was doing the darning when he
  walked to the porch with his
  newspaper.
The needle slipped when the front
  door slammed, and as I sucked the
  pain in my fingerpad I thought
  of the blood hues inside the
  plums and the hard seed
  in the fruit's centre that
  would play with my tongue all
  the next day and stave off heat's
  thirst.

I made dinner, cleaned dishes, brought
  in the laundry with the clothespins,
  pressed shirts, folded pants and
  hung them away in the closets as
  the last sliver of natural light
  slipped into the moon - full and
 cold and glowing and round like

  the plums
  that would have been my breakfast
  had I not fallen asleep before he did.

In the morning
  I found the
  note (on a
  leaf of
  prescription
  pad). I
  would have
  cried, but

  I could
  only wax
furniture.

Ways to Love: Monologues

Karen Alkalay-Gut

I

'There are many ways to love,'
says the professor with a birthmark
over half his face.
When he paces one way
he is almost handsome,
when he faces left
the red scar is exposed
and a monster leads the class.

'After the war I worked in a closed ward
for veterans: there was a little man -
shell-shocked, nervous, gay - who fell hard
for a big catatonic, and needed a way
to get his attention. One day he began
sitting next to him at meals and dripping
milk onto his thigh. It was a nice try,
but the catatonic didn't get the symbolism.'

I look around me in the lecture.
I am the only one not laughing.
The professor paces back and forth

II

There were days when she lay in bed
imagining a serious disease - something
that would make him feel guilty,
run to her bedside. Then
he would realise how much...

But at that point even she
could not keep up the fantasy;
he was not a standard man,
would never follow

a standard script. 'Oh,
sweet lover, that is why
I am in your thrall,
because you would not be swayed
even by my more drastic ploys.'

III

On days they had arranged to meet
he would sometimes wake from a dream
that he had been spread with honey
and now could not escape the flies.
For hours after he would catch himself
flicking away imaginary insects.

But he owed it to her, he'd say, the opportunity
to tell him what was in her heart.
After all she had contrived
everything for him, the luxurious flat,
the wondrous job he had always longed for,
the chance for fulfilment.
And all she appeared to demand in return
now that she seemed indifferent to caresses,
was his conversation.

Why she was so hungry for his presence
was a riddle - Lady - he wanted to shout
- it's over. Can't you let it rest?

IV

One night, I say, I will find out from where
this unrest ascends. I will let it go
as far out as it wants to pace, see the space
between accepted and haunted bonds.

My heart is caught like an escaped convict.
I am led, head down, back to propriety.

V

'Are you sure,'
she whispers into the evening,
'There is no chance for me?'

And I - in the kitchen,
white with flour and domesticity -
stop to contemplate her affinity
before I shake my head

VI

How many ways
are there, you ask,
the tortoise who tries always
to move forward even when heavy rocks
block your path. Every one of the women
you loved might have brought you joy
had you known to turn from the rocks.
Sometimes only the pressure
of your head against them
drove them to pace
like animals in cages
back and forth.

VII

Having one eye,
you look at me always
at an angle,
turn me this way and that,
examine it all.

We are in our patterned conjugal bed
shrieking in cacophonous unanimity.
It is both a death and quickening,
and then you roll away,
call out the name
of my god.

What Does A House Want?

Gary Geddes

A house has no unreasonable expectations
of travel or imperialist ambitions;
a house wants to stay
where it is.

A house does not demonstrate
against partition or harbour
grievances;
                a house is a safe
haven, anchorage, place
of rest.

Shut the door on excuses -
greed, political expediency.

A house remembers
its original inhabitants, ventures
comparisons:
                  the woman
tossing her hair
on a doorstep, the man
bent over his tools and patch
of garden.

What does a house want?

Laughter, sounds
of loving-making, to strengthen
the walls;
              a house
wants people, a permit
to persevere.

A house has no stones
to spare; no house has ever been convicted
of a felony, unless privacy

be considered a crime in the new
dispensation.

What does a house want?

Firm joints, things
on the level,
water rising in pipes.

Put out the eyes, forbid
the drama of exits,
entrances; somewhere
in the rubble a mechanism
leaks time,
                no place
familiar for a fly
to land
on.

Wheel Fever

May 1877

Connie Bensley

Frank Reynolds has ordered a *Coventry*,
48 inches high and with all
the new improvements.

But it cost £14, and I am afraid
to sink so much money - it would be almost
three months of my salary.

All my fellows in the village
have bicycle fever, and none
more than myself.

***

Rode on Aubrey's wooden cycle
into Warboys, to see a Spider-Wheel
which Monty has for sale.

But the tyres were tied on
with pieces of twine, so I did not
part with my cash.

***

I've done it! I could not bear to wait
any longer. I now possess a *Coventry*
(without the new improvements).

Before I paid, I took it for a spin
but lost the treadle,
landed in a heap

and had to have it taken back
in the cart, and put together.
But after that

89

I rode off round the lanes
as right as twelve o'clock
and pleased as Punch.

***

Coming back from a spin today, I met
Mr Dodds with his cartload of bread.
He must have known

that horses shy at bicycles, but
he didn't get down, and sure enough
his wretched animal

reared, backed into the dyke, and emptied
22 stone of bread and 6 stone of flour
into the water.

***

Set out with James Black, to ride
to the prayer meeting, but
by Redman's corner

he ran into me, knocked me off,
broke my handle, bent my treadle, and fell
on top of me.

***

I am receiving unpleasant letters from
Mr Dodds. I do not believe that flour
can be so dear.

Unlike Aubrey or Frank Reynolds,
I can now ride my bicycle
with arms folded.

***

I was riding my bicycle with my arms
folded on my way to Doddington,
when I hit a stone

and pitched on my head. Managed to get up
and stagger on, covered with blood
and feeling faint.

Of course I could not help Uncle
in the shop. The carrier put his pony in
and took me home.

***

Could not move this morning, so stiff
and sore. My bicycle will take three days
to put right.

I miss it dreadfully. Frank Reynolds
does not seem keen on the idea
of lending me his.

But I have had a carrot poultice put on
my eye and I shall soon be fit enough
to ride again.

Working the Bellows

Peter Gruffydd

Down, the ribbed air-bag
concertina'd seemed,
for a dusty instant, to snag.
Our backs tensed we gripped
the bar at knee-level, pulled
then Up, showering coal-motes
into flickering, dim light, it rose
sighing, sucked-in great, long
gulps of air until, full height
it paused to spew its rasping song
out into sunken furnace-light.

It needed, for what grave Mister
Price did with one hand a-dangle,
a three-strong evacuee muster
lined up by the bent, worn handle.
Bounced redly on the anvil
or spat grey from murky water-
buckets nearby, a tickling reek
of beaten, wetted iron clung.
The poised bellows, hung
in air like a leathery diver,
inched up a final creak.

Then down again, we hanging on
against the rise like drowning men,
to prove us worthy, until air's pressed
gout ran to shrinking fire which glowed
in the bellows exhaled grief.
A shire's bulk held up the roof,
his eye a new moon in shadow,
patiently allowed his hoof,
balanced in the smith's arm-hollow,
a trimming of its hard rind horn,
the curved blade a whetted blue.

While thirsty fire drank wheezy air
the bellows would droop and groan
at matter's need for loving care,
hiss and stoop with a calm moan
when the hazed grey horseshoe
was hammered to the shire's trim foot.
Slow, acrid curls of blue-burnt
smoke, swallowed in the chimney-soot
or lifted to black roof-timbers
by the cool, what doorway's draught
blurred over brick and cinders.

Enough, Price would glance; we'd stop.
With honour and work puffed out
we heard the ticking bellows drop.
The animal's warm, brown-coal mass
shifted, snickered gently,
and if the farmhand, loosely
holding its rope-halter, who'd rung
the dour smith's praises, might pass
a word to us or nod, we felt
a brotherhood, strong and patient,
working the bellows weighty lung.

Claimed by each night's closing latch,
we'd dream of daylight's swimming touch
on the forge-door's battered shiplap,
our stations in the nettles drift
beside a rusting plough and chains.
There we'd wait for the chinking slap
of worn-out shoes on the road,
remember the shire's wary, stumbled
exit, his tipping, in nervous pains,
of the cooled iron shoe's new load,
legs armoured in late sun's last rift.

One day the rumbly door stayed shut,
roof-top dark against a sky's far blue.
His heart, they said; that was the cut.
Within, the echoey chimney-flue,
squat bellows in chill, crack-lit

gloom, cold hearth, still horseshoe, tong,
anvil, hammer, the silent ground.
No more the smith's glanced command,
no pursed gaze when he chose long,
from mum bellow-workers round his door,
the day's air-masters, no more, no more.

About the Arvon Foundation

The Arvon Foundation administers three large houses: Lumb Bank in an isolated valley in the Pennines in West Yorkshire, Moniack Mhor, west of Inverness in the Highlands of Scotland, and Totleigh Barton in the middle of Devon.

Writing courses are run at each of these centres throughout the year. A course lasts for four and a half days and gives people of any age and background, who want to explore and practice imaginative writing (poetry, narrative, drama) the chance to live and work with two professional writers. The students must be ready to commit themselves, absolutely, to exploring whatever talent they might have. They have to work, to produce, to create. The professional writers set them to work then work with them.

Arvon draws on the whole pool of writers in this country and, since the first course in 1968, has employed over a thousand of them as tutors, the majority of whom have become constant supporters.

The Arvon Foundation is a registered Charity (Charity No. 306694) and receives a public subsidy from the Arts Council of England and from the Scottish Arts Council.

The first Arvon International Poetry Competition was held in 1980 with sponsorship from The Observer. The competition is now biennial. Anthologies from all previous poetry competitions are available from the Arvon Foundation.

For further information about the work of the Arvon Foundation, and its poetry competition, please contact:
The National Director,
Arvon Foundation,
Lumb Bank,
Heptonstall,
Hebden Bridge,
West Yorkshire,
HX7 6DF England.

Poets, Prizes and Special Commendations

97